Trace each letter. Use this page as reference.

Aa Bb Cc Dd

Ee Ff Gg Hh

Ii Jj Kk Ll Mm

Nn Oo Pp Qq

Rr Ss Tt Uu Vv

Ww Xx Yy Zz

Read the letters and the animal name. Color the animal.

A a   alligator

   CD-104329

Trace and write the letters.

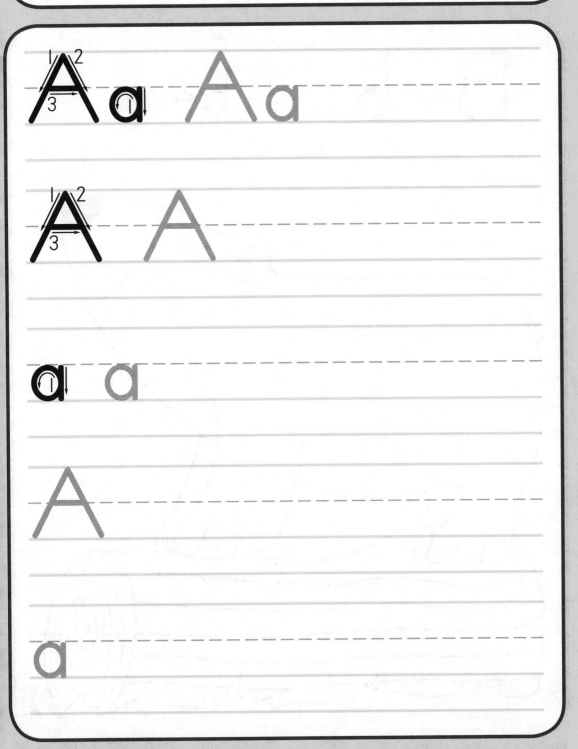

Read the letters and the animal name. Color the animal.

B b   bear

CD-104329   © Carson-Dellosa

Trace and write the letters.

B̲b̲ B̲b̲ -

B̲ B̲ -

b̲ b̲ -

B̲ -

b̲ -

  CD-104329

Read the letters and the animal name. Color the animal.

C c   camel

CD-104329   © Carson-Dellosa

Trace and write the letters.

C c   C c

C   C

c   c

C

c

Read the letters and the animal name. Color the animal.

D d   dinosaur

Trace and write the letters.

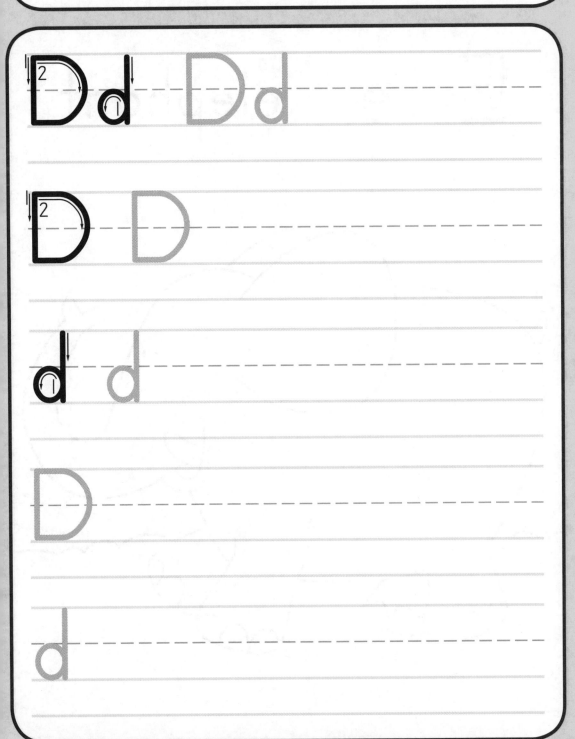

CD-104329

Read the letters and the animal name. Color the animal.

E e 2 3 4   elephant

   CD-104329

Trace and write the letters.

E e   E e

E E

e   e

E

e

Read the letters and the animal name. Color the animal.

F f

fish

CD-104329

Trace and write the letters.

Read the letters and the animal name. Color the animal.

G g   goat

CD-104329

Trace and write the letters.

G g   G g

G   G

g   g

G

g

Read the letters and the animal name. Color the animal.

H h

horse

 CD-104329

Trace and write the letters.

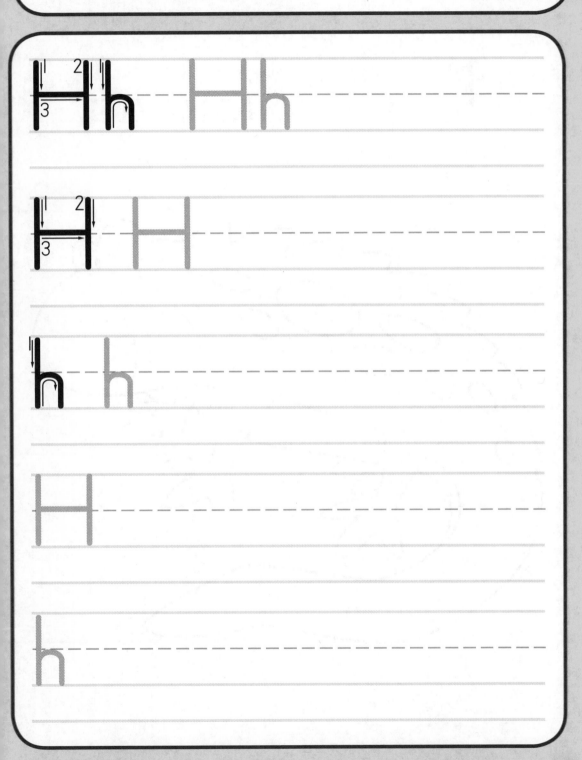

Read the letters and the animal name. Color the animal.

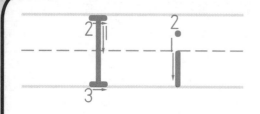

iguana

CD-104329

Trace and write the letters.

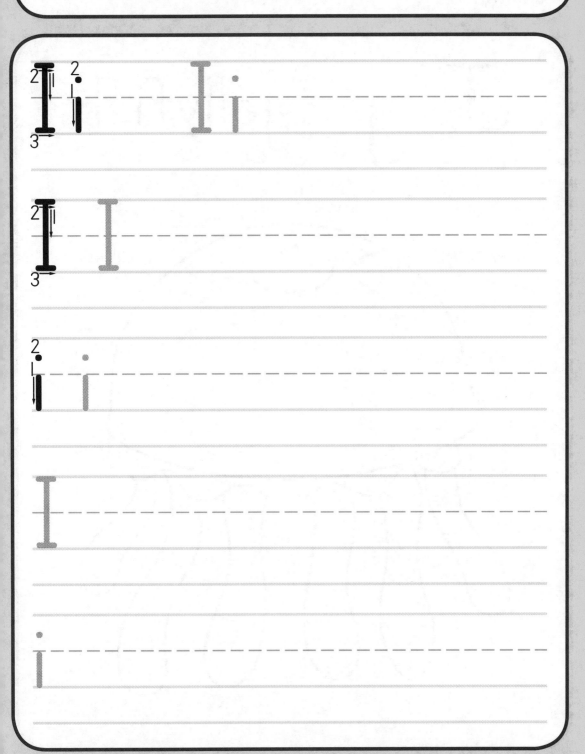

Read the letters and the animal name. Color the animal.

J j jellyfish

CD-104329

Trace and write the letters.

Read the letters and the animal name. Color the animal.

K K² k k² kangaroo

CD-I04329

Trace and write the letters.

Read the letters and the animal name. Color the animal.

L l

lion

CD-104329 © Carson-Dellosa

Trace and write the letters.

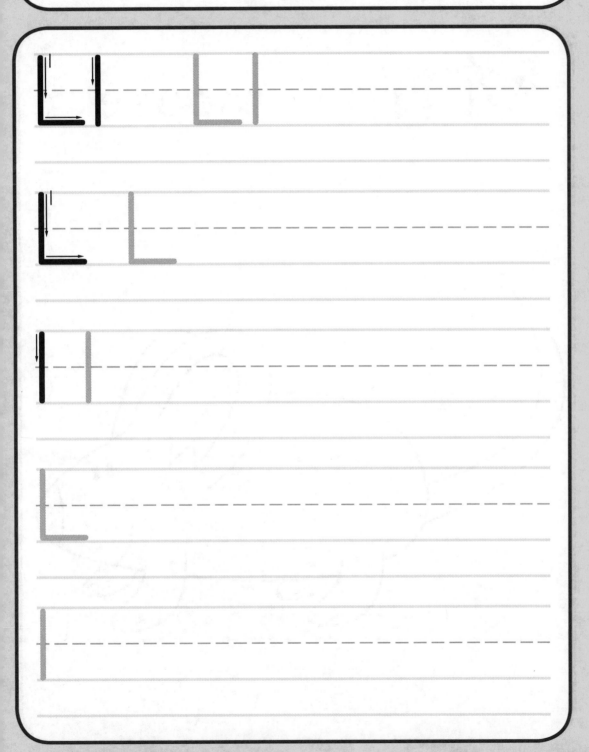

Read the letters and the animal name. Color the animal.

M m   mouse

CD-104329

Trace and write the letters.

N n   newt

Trace and write the letters.

Read the letters and the animal name. Color the animal.

O o

owl

CD-104329 © Carson-Dellosa

Trace and write the letters.

P p   penguin

Trace and write the letters.

Read the letters and the animal name. Color the animal.

Q q   quail

CD-104329

Trace and write the letters.

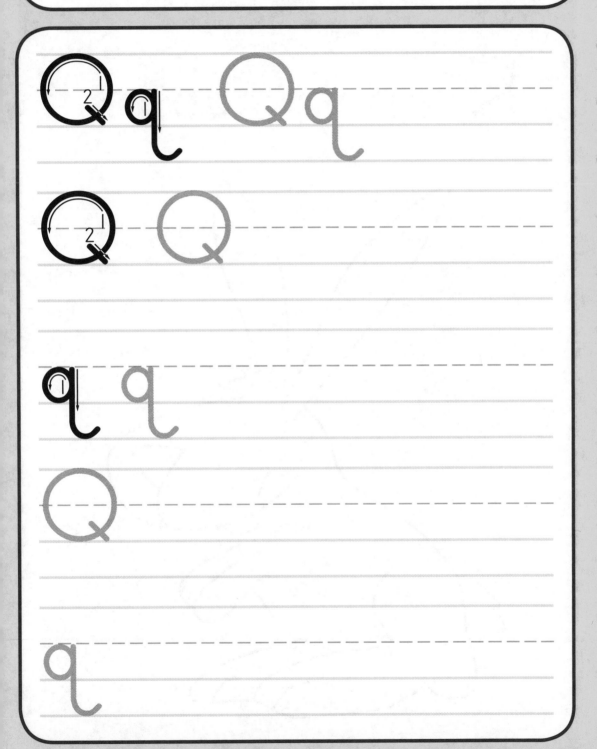

Read the letters and the animal name. Color the animal.

R r   rabbit

   CD-104329

Trace and write the letters.

Read the letters and the animal name. Color the animal.

S s

seal

CD-104329

Trace and write the letters.

S s   S s

S   S

s   s

S

s

Read the letters and the animal name. Color the animal.

turtle

Trace and write the letters.

Read the letters and the animal name. Color the animal.

U u   unicorn

   CD-104329

Trace and write the letters.

Read the letters and the animal name. Color the animal.

V v

vulture

CD-104329

Trace and write the letters.

Read the letters and the animal name. Color the animal.

W w   walrus

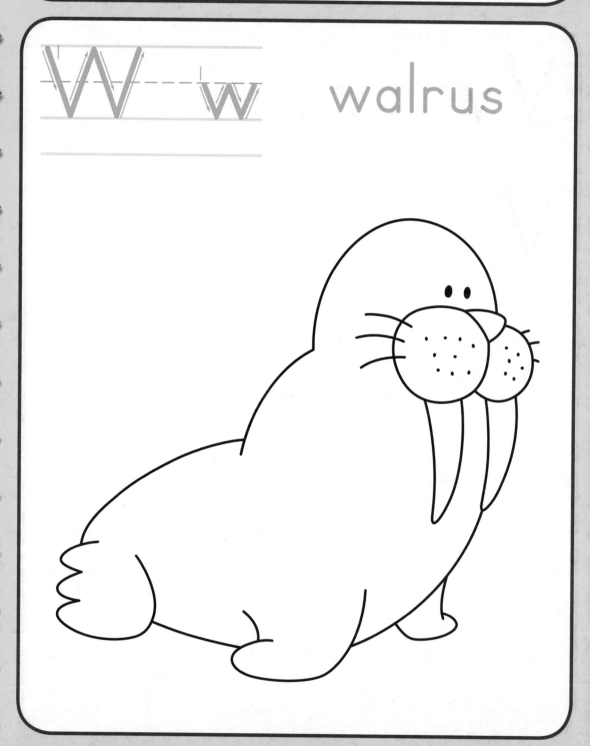

CD-104329   © Carson-Dellosa

Trace and write the letters.

 CD-104329

Read the letters and the animal name. Color the animal.

X x

fo<u>x</u>

CD-104329

Trace and write the letters.

Read the letters and the animal name. Color the animal.

Y y

yak

CD-104329 © Carson-Dellosa

Trace and write the letters.

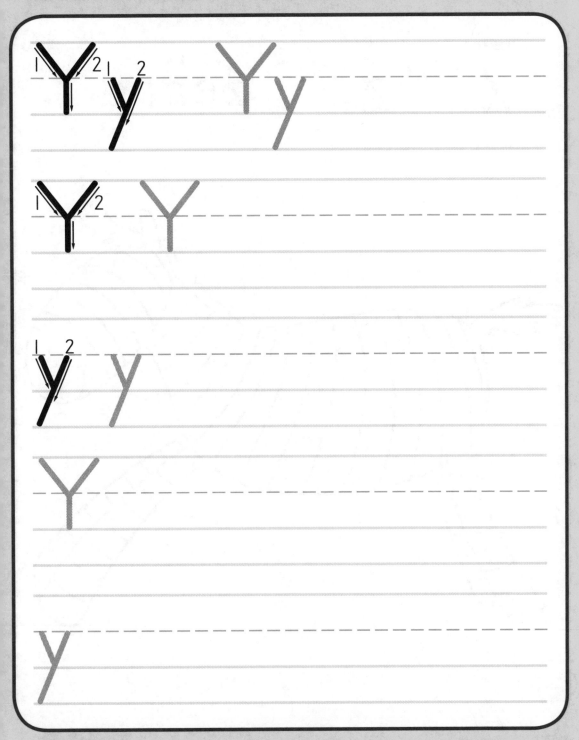

Read the letters and the animal name. Color the animal.

Z z   zebra

Trace and write the letters.

Z z   Z z

Z   Z

z z   z

Z

z

Practice tracing the letters.

Aa   Bb   Cc

Dd   Ee   Ff

Gg   Hh   Ii

Jj   Kk   Ll

Mm   Nn

Practice tracing the letters.

Oo Pp Qq

Rr Ss Tt

Uu Vv Ww

Xx Yy

Zz

Connect the dots from A to Z. Start at the ★.
Color the picture.

CD-104329   © Carson-Dellosa

Connect the dots from A to Z. Start at the ★. Color the picture.

CD-104329 **57**

Draw a line to match each uppercase letter to the correct lowercase letter.

CD-104329

Draw a line to match each uppercase letter to the correct lowercase letter.

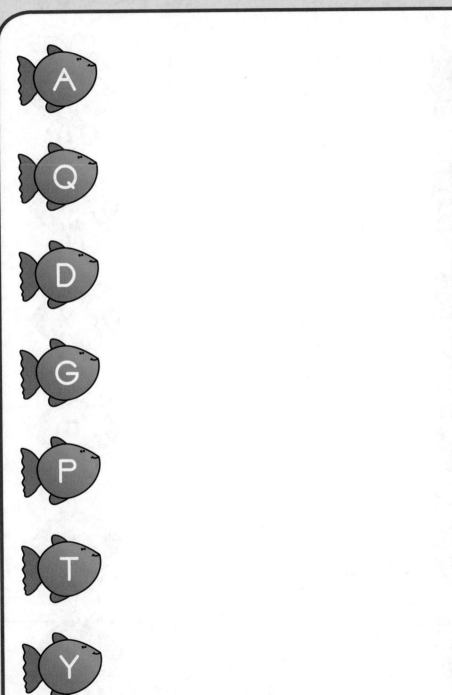

Draw a line to match each uppercase letter to the correct lowercase letter.

Draw a line to match each uppercase letter to the correct lowercase letter.

 K

 l

 L

 i

 O

 j

 Z

 o

 I

 k

 J

 z

 CD-104329

Say the name of each animal. Circle the letter with the same beginning sound.

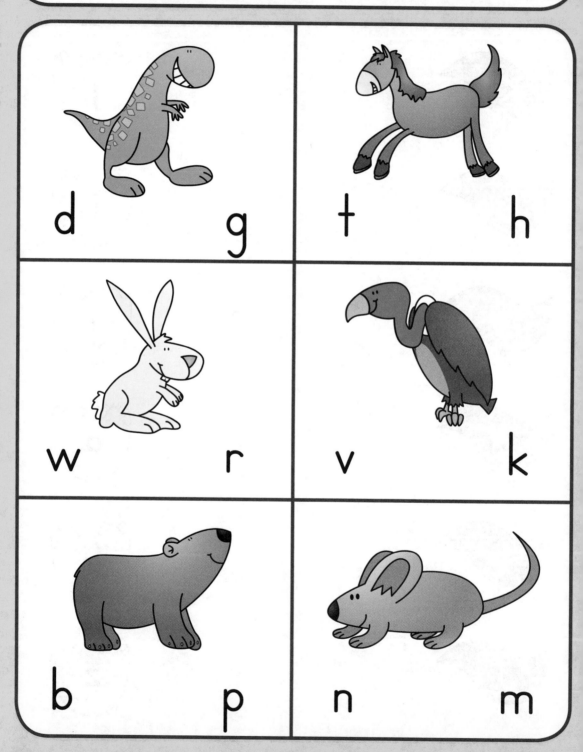

d   g   t   h

w   r   v   k

b   p   n   m

CD-104329

Say the name of each animal. Circle the letter with the same beginning sound.

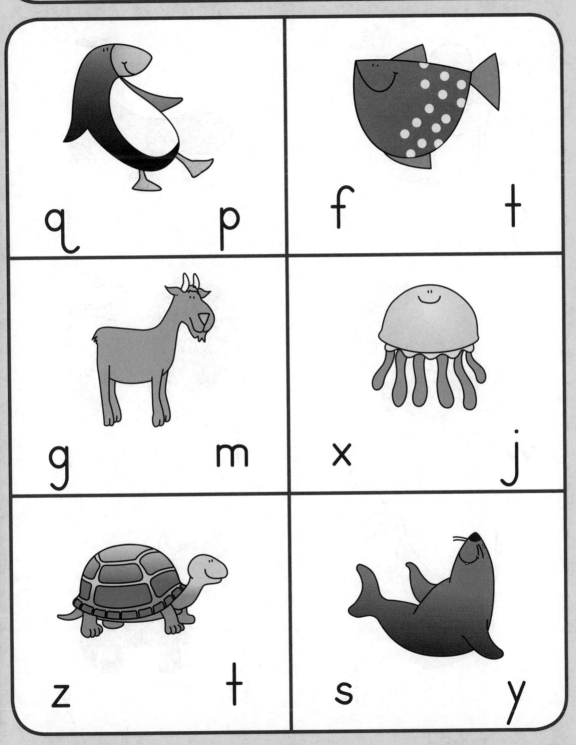

q   p   f   t

g   m   x   j

z   t   s   y

    CD-104329   **63**

Say the name of each animal. Circle the letter with the same beginning sound.

c   x

v   n

w   y

l   r

z   k

h   y

CD-104329   © Carson-Dellosa